PEGAN

SMOOTHIES

Better Health, High Energy, and Weight Loss

I0176821

Rae Lynde

www.PeganPantry.com

Ordinary Matters Publishing
All Rights Reserved

PEGAN SMOOTHIES
Better Health, High Energy, and Weight Loss
Ordinary Matters Publishing
Ordinary MattersPublishing.com

Book Layout © 2014 BookDesignTemplates.com

PEGAN SMOOTHIES / Rae Lynde--1st Ed.
ASIN: B01M7QKJ0A (eBook)
ISBN-10: 1-941303-26-9 (print)
ISBN-13: 978-1-941303-26-9 (print)

www.PeganPantry.com

www.facebook.com/PeganPantry

"No matter how old you are, no matter how much you weigh, you can still control the health of your body."

—DR. OZ

CONTENTS

ABOUT SMOOTHIES..9

What Are Smoothies? 9

What Are Their Benefits? 9

Why are Pegan smoothies good for you? 10

What equipment do you need? 11

How to get started.. 11

PEGAN DIET BASICS 13

Five Health Benefits of the Pegan Diet....................14

Eight Ways to Avoid or Reduce Animal Fat............. 14

What you Need to Do for Smoothies 16

WHY I LOVE PEGAN 1

SMOOTHIE RECIPES... 5

FRUIT SMOOTHIES... 9

Refreshing Raspberry Smoothie........................ 9

Terrific Triple Berry Blend 11

Tropical Mango Pineapple Smoothie 12

Bountiful Blueberry Mint Blend...................... 13

Peachy Pear Mango Smoothie.......................... 14

Sweet Strawberry Kiwi Smoothie 15

Double Berry Blast with Coconut 16

Bright Carrot Cucumber and Pear Smoothie 17

GREEN SMOOTHIES.. 21

Sassy Spinach Green Apple Smoothie..........................21

Spinach Avocado Lime Cooler 23

Celery Cucumber and Kale Smoothie 24

Gorgeous Green Grape Smoothie 25

Zippy Zucchini Kiwi Smoothie 26

Cucumber Kale Green Smoothie...................................27

Broccoli Cucumber Blast...28

Invigorating Kiwi Kale Smoothie.................................29

Celery Spinach and Cucumber Smoothie 30

BANANA SMOOTHIES...33

Simple Strawberry Banana Smoothie 33

Coco-Nutty Banana Smoothie 35

Easy Almond Butter Banana Smoothie 36

Bangin' Banana Yogurt Smoothie................................37

Perfect Pineapple Banana Smoothie 38

Blueberry Banana Blend with Lime 39

PROTEIN SMOOTHIES 43

Choco-Coconut Protein Shake 43

Smooth Strawberry Yogurt Protein Shake..................45

Chocolate Banana Walnut Protein Shake....................46

Cinnamon Almond Protein Shake 47

Creamy Orange Dream Protein Shake 48

Almond Butter Banana Protein Shake.........................49

THERAPEUTIC SMOOTHIES..53

Rejuvenating Romaine Raspberry Smoothie..............53

Pick-Me-Up Peach Mango Smoothie.......... 55

Immune-Boosting Smoothie.......... 57

Calming Cherry Pomegranate Smoothie.......... 59

Almond and Green Tea Smoothie.......... 60

Revitalizing Raspberry Cucumber Smoothie.......... 61

Energizing Avocado Lime Smoothie.......... 62

Soothing Cucumber Cantaloupe Cooler.......... 63

Super Healthy Smoothie.......... 64

FUN SMOOTHIES.......... 67

Awesome Apple Ginger Beet Smoothie.......... 67

Merry Mango and Ginger Refresher.......... 69

Cinnamon Pumpkin Pie Smoothie.......... 70

Creamy Cranberry Cinnamon Smoothie.......... 71

Wacky Watermelon Refresher.......... 72

Velvety Vanilla Almond Smoothie.......... 73

Crazy Cucumber Melon Cooler.......... 74

Blackberry Yogurt Smoothie with Mint.......... 75

CONCLUSION.......... 79

Yes, You've Done It!.......... 81

Get Your Free Pegan Food Pantry Checklist.......... 81

My Pegan Diet Cookbooks:.......... 83

About the Author.......... 87

Enjoyed this Cookbook?.......... 89

NOTES.......... 91

INDEX.......... 107

ABOUT SMOOTHIES

What Are Smoothies?

Smoothies are blended drinks made predominately from fruits. However, they can also be made from leafy green vegetables. Many people add soy or almond milk, nut milks, various nut butters and even dairy-free yogurts to their smoothies.

What Are Their Benefits?

You'll find many health benefits to drinking smoothies and you can expect to experience at least some of these:

Improved hydration – smoothies are full of water, from the fruits and veggies to the dairy products, which are largely water. Drinking a smoothie for breakfast is a good way to ensure that you start the day fully hydrated.

Increased energy, focus and mental clarity – increasing your intake for fruits and vegetables will leave you with bags of energy. In turn, this will lead to increased focus and mental clarity. No more brain fog!

Better sleep – a body that is well hydrated and full of the right nutrition, functions in a better way. This includes sleep.

Release of toxins – giving the body good nutrition, in an easily assimilable form, such as liquids, allows it time to 'clean house' and release toxins that have built up over time.

Improved digestion and bowel movements – eating a natural diet that is full of fruits, vegetables and fiber, means that our digestive systems work better, and our bowel movements become more regular.

Better immune system – eating a diet that is full of essential nutrients, vitamins and anti-oxidants, ensures our immune systems are working to the best of their ability. You can expect less colds, bugs and infections when eating this way.

Why are Pegan smoothies good for you?

Many smoothies on the market today are made from fruit concentrates, syrups and added sugars, preservatives and flavorings.

Pegan smoothies follow the dietary principles laid out by the Pegan diet. No sugar-filled concentrates, syrups, or preservatives. Clean eating is emphasized. Fresh is definitely best, and with a Pegan smoothie you are guaranteed goodness with none of those nasty ingredients.

What equipment do you need?

All you need to make smoothies is a blender, or a smoothie maker. If you use a blender, make sure it has a 2-3 liter jug on it. Note, the higher the speed of your blender, the easier it will be to completely blend your smoothies.

How to get started

Simply make sure you have a good variety of fruits, soy or almond milk, and leafy green vegetables to hand. Best to buy organic produce where possible. A good starting point would be to have:

At least 6 oranges.
Spinach or Kale.
A selection of fruits and berries.
Dairy-free milk, soy, plant-based, or almond.
Dairy-free yogurt.

PEGAN DIET BASICS

The Pegan Diet is all about clean eating. The Pegan diet is *not* a vegan diet. Vegans seek to completely eradicate animal fat from their diet. In the Pegan diet you want to greatly reduce the level of animal fat that you take in on a daily basis. However, many who are on the Pegan diet do take advantage of the great vegan recipes that are readily available. The difference is that they also make use of Paleo diet and other recipes that fall under the Pegan guidelines and have a *limited* meat component.

For the confirmed Paleo and pure Vegan dietary adopters, I doubt this diet will fully satisfy either one. Because of the inclusion of meat, vegans will say this is not a truly inspired vegan diet. For avid Paleo dieters, But for many people, the Pegan diet is a wonderful pathway leading to a healthy and flexible dietary lifestyle.

The Pegan Diet minimizes risk. Gone are the added sugars, dairy, gluten, processed foods, refined oils and heavy reliance on meat. All of them contribute to inflammation. So if you want to reduce inflammation, go Pegan. If you want to reduce stress, adapt your eating habits to conform to the Pegan lifestyle.

Five Health Benefits of the Pegan Diet

1) Rich in nutrients including vitamins and minerals
2) Low in antibiotics, hormones, and pesticides
3) Very low glycemic load (no grains or refined sugar)
4) High in healthy fats (avocado, olive oil, nuts, etc.)
5) May be lower in calories than standard diets

Eight Ways to Avoid or Reduce Animal Fat

While I don't completely avoid animal fat, I do use a number of "vegan" products to help lower amount of animal fat I consume daily.

Vegan-marked products are much more easily found in regular grocery stores than ever before. I often find these products in either the produce section, a natural or "whole foods" aisle or area, or in a special section in the cooler dairy area. You must find the word "vegan" on the container to make sure what you are buying is completely free of animal fat.

Here are some ways that I have successfully managed to make that happen.

1) Substitute "vegan" butter instead of the usual butter or margarine.

2) Substitute coconut oil for oils that contain animal fat.

3) Substitute "vegan" mayonnaise for the regular mayo you get from the grocery store.

4) Substitute avocado oil when coating a baked potato.

5) Substitute "vegan" sour cream for regular sour cream.

6) Substitute "vegan" cheese for your regular shredded cheese.

7) Eliminate all animal fat for one meal per day.

8) Have an occasional no-meat day.

For more information on the Pegan Diet, check out my book *Pegan for Beginners: Breakfast, Lunch, and Dinner Recipes* where you'll find 45 delicious, mouth-watering recipes.

What you Need to Do for Smoothies

When you are choosing the ingredients for your smoothies, make sure you select the right ingredients.

1) No processed grains, refined sugars, dairy products, or packaged foods.
2) Use fresh, wholesome foods like fruits and vegetables, nuts, seeds, and avocado.
3) Avoid gluten.
4) Avoid dairy products
5) Focus on using mostly plant-based foods.

Additional Notes
Use this section to make additional notes.

_____

_____

_____

_____

_____

WHY I LOVE PEGAN

Pegan. It's a strange-sounding word, isn't it? I know the first time I heard it in early 2015, I thought it was an odd name for a diet. After a little investigation, I found it is the result of combining the best principles of two diets: Pegan and Vegan. Pegan eating with a growing emphasis on clean eating is a natural marriage of food that works for my lifestyle. In general, I lean toward eating less meat and favor added vegetables and fruits.

I don't metabolize meat as fast as other foods so I gain weight when I eat heavy meat-laden meals. The pounds drop off as soon as I switch back to my more natural dietary habit of reduced meat and more vegetables and fruit.

For most vegans, this is the most controversial aspect of the idea of combining Paleo and Vegan diets. No animal fats are the mainstay of the vegan diet. True vegans will not embrace this diet. But for those who appreciate and value the vegan and vegetarian lifestyle but prefer to ensure that they have some meat in their diet, Pegan is a good option.

Wean yourself off from Dairy and Gluten

More and more people, either by choice or necessity, are moving towards dairy and gluten-free diets. For most, the choice comes from the health benefits they receive when they eliminate dairy and gluten food.

Moving toward a diet free of dairy and gluten food is easier than ever. Gluten-free breads, crackers, and even cake mixes are easily found in most grocery stores. Dairy-free products are also easily discovered, too. Almond milk, coconut milk, and many other dairy-free milk substitutes are available.

I try to focus on what I can have. I encourage you to spend more time learning about all the wonderful foods you do have that will enhance your life and your health.

When it comes to smoothies, you'll be delighted with your choices. Turn the page and give these delicious recipes a try.

SMOOTHIE RECIPES

The following recipes offer a wide variety of breakfast, lunch, dinner, and dessert recipes. Nutritional information is provided at the end of each recipe.

NOTE: Most recipes make one large smoothie or can be divided into two.

B

FRUIT SMOOTHIES

Refreshing Raspberry Smoothie

Servings: 1 to 2

Ingredients:
2 cups frozen raspberries
1 cup fresh squeezed orange juice
1/2 cup coconut yogurt
1/2 cup ice cubes
1 teaspoon honey

Instructions:
Combine the ingredients in a high-speed blender.

Blend the mixture on high speed for 30 to 60 seconds until thoroughly combined.

Pour the smoothie into glasses and enjoy immediately.

Nutritional Information:
390 calories per serving, 2g fat, 94g carbs, 4g protein, 11g fiber

Additional Notes
Use this section to make additional notes.

_____

_____

_____

_____

_____

_____

_____

_____

Terrific Triple Berry Blend

Servings: 1 to 2

Ingredients:
1 cup frozen sliced strawberries
1/2 cup frozen raspberries
1/2 cup frozen blueberries
1 small frozen banana, peeled and sliced
3/4 cups unsweetened almond milk
1.4 cup coconut yogurt
1 tablespoon chia seeds

Instructions:
Combine the ingredients in a high-speed blender.

Blend the mixture on high speed for 30 to 60 seconds until thoroughly combined.

Pour the smoothie into glasses and enjoy immediately.

Nutritional Information:
260 calories per serving, 7g fat, 47g carbs, 6g protein, 11.5g fiber

Tropical Mango Pineapple Smoothie

Servings: 1 to 2

Ingredients:
1 cup frozen chopped pineapple
1/2 cup frozen chopped mango
1 small frozen banana, peeled and chopped
1 cup fresh squeezed orange juice
1/2 cup ice cubes
1 tablespoon fresh lemon juice
1 teaspoon honey

Instructions:
Combine the ingredients in a high-speed blender.

Blend the mixture on high speed for 30 to 60 seconds until thoroughly combined.

Pour the smoothie into glasses and enjoy immediately.

Nutritional Information:
200 calories per serving, 0g fat, 50g carbs, 2g protein, 5g fiber

Bountiful Blueberry Mint Blend

Servings: 1 to 2

Ingredients:
1 1/2 cups frozen blueberries
1 small frozen banana, peeled and sliced
1 cup unsweetened almond milk
1/2 cup coconut yogurt
1/2 cup ice cubes
2 to 3 tablespoons fresh chopped mint

Instructions:
Combine the ingredients in a high-speed blender.

Blend the mixture on high speed for 30 to 60 seconds until thoroughly combined.

Pour the smoothie into glasses and enjoy immediately.

Nutritional Information:
160 calories per serving, 3g fat, 32g carbs, 3g protein, 5g fiber

Peachy Pear Mango Smoothie

Servings: 1 to 2

Ingredients
1 cup frozen sliced peaches
1/2 cup frozen chopped mango
1 ripe pear, cored and chopped
1 cup coconut water
2 tablespoons chia seeds
1 teaspoon honey

Instructions:
Combine the ingredients in a high-speed blender.

Blend the mixture on high speed for 30 to 60 seconds until thoroughly combined.

Pour the smoothie into glasses and enjoy immediately.

Nutritional Information:
280 calories per serving, 9.5g fat, 22g carbs, 6.5g protein, 14g fiber

Sweet Strawberry Kiwi Smoothie

Servings: 1 to 2

Ingredients:
2 cups frozen sliced strawberries
1 ripe kiwifruit, peeled and sliced
1/2 small seedless cucumber, chopped
1 cup coconut water
1/2 cup ice cubes
1 tablespoon wheatgrass powder
1 teaspoon honey

Instructions:
Combine the ingredients in a high-speed blender.

Blend the mixture on high speed for 30 to 60 seconds until thoroughly combined.

Pour the smoothie into glasses and enjoy immediately.

Nutritional Information:
155 calories per serving, 0g fat, 34g carbs, 4g protein, 6g fiber

Double Berry Blast with Coconut

Servings: 1 to 2

Ingredients:
1 1/2 cup frozen blueberries
1 cup frozen sliced strawberries
1 cup coconut water
1/2 cup coconut yogurt
1/2 cup ice cubes
1 tablespoon fresh lemon juice

Instructions:
Combine the ingredients in a high speed blender.

Blend the mixture on high speed for 30 to 60 seconds until thoroughly combined.
Pour the smoothie into glasses and enjoy immediately.

Nutritional Information:
150 calories per serving, 1.5g fat, 33g carbs, 2.5g protein, 4g fiber

Bright Carrot Cucumber and Pear Smoothie

Servings: 1 to 2

Ingredients:
2 medium carrots, peeled and sliced
1 small seedless cucumber, diced
1 ripe pear, cored and chopped
1 cup unsweetened apple juice
1/2 cup ice cubes
1 teaspoon fresh grated ginger

Instructions:
Combine the ingredients in a high-speed blender.

Blend the mixture on high speed for 30 to 60 seconds until thoroughly combined.

Pour the smoothie into glasses and enjoy.

Nutritional Information:
150 calories per serving, 0.5g fat, 37g carbs, 2g protein, 4.5g fiber

Additional Notes

Use this section to make additional notes.

_____

_____

_____

_____

_____

_____

_____

_____

_____

_____

_____

GREEN SMOOTHIES

Sassy Spinach Green Apple Smoothie

Servings: 1 to 2

Ingredients:
2 cups fresh baby spinach, chopped
1 medium green apple, cored and chopped
1 small stalk celery, chopped
1 cup coconut water
1/2 cup ice cubes
1 tablespoon wheatgrass powder

Instructions:
Combine the ingredients in a high speed blender.

Blend the mixture on high speed for 30 to 60 seconds until thoroughly combined.

Pour the smoothie into glasses and enjoy immediately.

Nutritional Information:

120 calories per serving, 0g fat, 27.5g carbs, 4g protein, 6g fiber

Additional Notes

Use this section to make additional notes.

_____

_____

_____

_____

_____

_____

_____

_____

Spinach Avocado Lime Cooler

Servings: 1 to 2

Ingredients:
1 1/2 cups fresh baby spinach, chopped
1 medium ripe avocado, pitted and chopped
1/2 cup seedless cucumber, chopped
1 cup water
1/2 cup ice cubes
2 tablespoons fresh lime juice
1 teaspoon fresh lime zest

Instructions:
Combine the ingredients in a high speed blender.

Blend the mixture on high speed for 30 to 60 seconds until thoroughly combined.

Pour the smoothie into glasses and top with fresh lime zest.

Nutritional Information:
225 calories per serving, 20g fat, 14g carbs, 3g protein, 8g fiber

Celery Cucumber and Kale Smoothie

Servings: 1 to 2

Ingredients:
1 1/2 cups fresh chopped kale
1 small seedless cucumber, chopped
1 medium stalk celery, sliced
1 cup unsweetened apple juice
1/2 cup ice cubes
1 tablespoon ground flaxseed
1 teaspoon honey

Instructions:
Combine the ingredients in a high speed blender.

Blend the mixture on high speed for 30 to 60 seconds until thoroughly combined.

Pour the smoothie into glasses and enjoy immediately.

Nutritional Information:
120 calories per serving, 1g fat, 26g carbs, 3g protein, 2.5g fiber

Gorgeous Green Grape Smoothie

Servings: 1 to 2

Ingredients:
2 cups green seedless grapes
1/2 cup seedless cucumber, chopped
1 large stalk celery, sliced
1 1/2 cups ice cubes
1 cup unsweetened grape juice
1 tablespoon fresh chopped parsley

Instructions:
Combine the ingredients in a high speed blender.

Blend the mixture on high speed for 30 to 60 seconds until thoroughly combined.

Pour the smoothie into glasses and enjoy immediately.

Nutritional Information:
150 calories per serving, 0.5g fat, 38g carbs, 1g protein, 1.5g fiber

Zippy Zucchini Kiwi Smoothie

Servings: 1 to 2

Ingredients:
2 ripe kiwifruit, peeled and sliced
1 small zucchini, peeled and chopped
1 cup unsweetened apple juice
1/2 cup ice cubes
1 teaspoon honey (optional)

Instructions:
Combine the ingredients in a high speed blender.

Blend the mixture on high speed for 30 to 60 seconds until thoroughly combined.

Pour the smoothie into glasses and enjoy immediately.

Nutritional Information:
130 calories per serving, 1g fat, 31g carbs, 2g protein, 3g fiber

Cucumber Kale Green Smoothie

Servings: 1 to 2

Ingredients:
1 1/2 cups fresh chopped kale
1 cup seedless cucumber, diced
1 stalk celery, sliced thin
1 cup coconut water
1/2 cup ice cubes
1 tablespoon fresh lime juice

Instructions:
Combine the ingredients in a high speed blender.

Blend the mixture on high speed for 30 to 60 seconds until thoroughly combined.

Pour the smoothie into glasses and enjoy immediately.

Nutritional Information:
70 calories per serving, 0g fat, 17g carbs, 2g protein, 1g fiber

Broccoli Cucumber Blast

Servings: 1 to 2

Ingredients:
2 cups frozen broccoli florets
1/2 cup seedless cucumber, diced
1/2 medium frozen banana, peeled and sliced
1 cup water
1/2 cup unsweetened almond milk

Instructions:
Combine the ingredients in a high speed blender.

Blend the mixture on high speed for 30 to 60 seconds until thoroughly combined.

Pour the smoothie into glasses and enjoy immediately.

Nutritional Information:
70 calories per serving, 1g fat, 12.5g carbs, 2g protein, 3.5g fiber

Invigorating Kiwi Kale Smoothie

Servings: 1 or 2

Ingredients:
2 cups fresh chopped kale
2 ripe kiwifruit, peeled and sliced
1 1/2 cups coconut water
1/2 cup ice cubes
1 tablespoon fresh lemon juice
1 teaspoon coconut oil

Instructions:
Combine the ingredients in a high speed blender.

Blend the mixture on high speed for 30 to 60 seconds until thoroughly combined.

Pour the smoothie into glasses and enjoy immediately.

Nutritional Information:
150 calories per serving, 3g fat, 30.5g carbs, 3g protein, 3g fiber

Celery Spinach and Cucumber Smoothie

Servings: 1 to 2

Ingredients:
2 cups fresh baby spinach, chopped
1 cup seedless cucumber, diced
1 cup frozen chopped pineapple
1 medium stalk celery, sliced
1 cup water
1 teaspoon honey (optional)

Instructions:
Combine the ingredients in a high speed blender.

Blend the mixture on high speed for 30 to 60 seconds until thoroughly combined.

Pour the smoothie into glasses and enjoy immediately.

Nutritional Information:
85 calories per serving, 0g fat, 21g carbs, 2g protein, 3.5g fiber

BANANA SMOOTHIES

Simple Strawberry Banana Smoothie

Servings: 1 to 2

Ingredients:

1 1/2 cups frozen sliced strawberries
1 medium frozen banana, peeled and sliced
1 cup unsweetened almond milk
1/2 cup coconut yogurt
1 teaspoon raw honey, local if possible
Pinch ground cinnamon

Instructions:

Combine the ingredients in a high speed blender.

Blend the mixture on high speed for 30 to 60 seconds until thoroughly combined.

Pour the smoothie into glasses and enjoy immediately.

Nutritional Information:

140 calories per serving, 3g fat, 27g carbs, 3g protein, 4g fiber

Additional Notes

Use this section to make additional notes.

_____

_____

_____

_____

_____

_____

_____

Coco-Nutty Banana Smoothie

Servings: 1 to 2

Ingredients:

2 medium frozen bananas, peeled and chopped
1 1/2 cups unsweetened coconut milk beverage
1.2 cup coconut yogurt
2 tablespoons shredded unsweetened coconut
2 tablespoons chopped almonds
2 to 3 drops almond extract

Instructions:

Combine the ingredients in a high speed blender.

Blend the mixture on high speed for 30 to 60 seconds until thoroughly combined.

Pour the smoothie into glasses and enjoy immediately.

Nutritional Information:

220 calories per serving, 8g fat, 34g carbs, 4g protein, 6g fiber

Easy Almond Butter Banana Smoothie

Servings: 1 to 2

Ingredients:

2 medium frozen bananas, peeled and sliced
1 1/2 cups unsweetened almond milk
1/2 cup coconut yogurt
2 tablespoons smooth almond butter
Pinch ground cinnamon
Pinch ground nutmeg

Instructions:

Combine the ingredients in a high speed blender.

Blend the mixture on high speed for 30 to 60 seconds until thoroughly combined.

Pour the smoothie into glasses and enjoy immediately.

Nutritional Information:

260 calories per serving, 12g fat, 6g carbs, 6.5g protein, 2g fiber

Bangin' Banana Yogurt Smoothie

Servings: 1 to 2

Ingredients:

2 medium frozen bananas, peeled and sliced
1 1/2 cups coconut yogurt
1 cup unsweetened almond milk
1/2 cup ice cubes

Instructions:

Combine the ingredients in a high speed blender.

Blend the mixture on high speed for 30 to 60 seconds until thoroughly combined.

Pour the smoothie into glasses and enjoy immediately.

Nutritional Information:

215 calories per serving, 5g fat, 40g carbs, 5g protein, 5g fiber

Perfect Pineapple Banana Smoothie

Servings: 1 to 2

Ingredients:

1 1/2 cups frozen chopped pineapple
1 large frozen banana, peeled and sliced
1 cup fresh-squeezed orange juice
1 cup ice cubes
1 teaspoon fresh lemon juice

Instructions:

Combine the ingredients in a high-speed blender.

Blend the mixture on high speed for 30 to 60 seconds until thoroughly combined.

Pour the smoothie into glasses and enjoy immediately.

Nutritional Information:

200 calories per serving, 0.5g fat, 49g carbs, 1.5g protein, 4.5g fiber

Blueberry Banana Blend with Lime

Servings: 1 to 2

Ingredients:

1 1/2 cups frozen blueberries
1 large frozen banana, peeled and sliced
1 1/2 cups coconut water
1/2 cup ice cubes
2 tablespoons fresh lime juice
1 teaspoon fresh lime zest

Instructions:

Combine the ingredients in a high-speed blender.

Blend the mixture on high speed for 30 to 60 seconds until thoroughly combined.

Pour the smoothie into glasses and enjoy immediately.

Nutritional Information:

175 calories per serving, 0.5g fat, 45g carbs, 1.5g protein, 5g fiber

Additional Notes

Use this section to make additional notes.

_____

_____

_____

_____

_____

_____

_____

_____

_____

_____

_____

_____

PROTEIN SMOOTHIES

Choco-Coconut Protein Shake

Servings: 1 to 2

Ingredients:

2 medium frozen bananas, peeled and sliced
1 1/2 cups unsweetened almond milk
1/2 cup canned coconut
1 scoop chocolate protein powder
3 to 4 tablespoons unsweetened shredded coconut
1 teaspoon coconut oil

Instructions:

Combine the ingredients in a high-speed blender

Blend on high speed for 30 to 60 seconds until smooth and well combined.

Pour the smoothie into glasses and enjoy immediately.

Nutritional Information:

360 calories per serving, 23g fat, 36g carbs, 9g protein, 8g fiber

Additional Notes
Use this section to make additional notes.

_____

_____

_____

_____

_____

_____

_____

Smooth Strawberry Yogurt Protein Shake

Servings: 1 to 2

Ingredients:

1 1/2 cups frozen sliced strawberries
1 cup coconut yogurt
1/2 cup unsweetened almond milk
1/2 cup ice cubes
1 scoop plain protein powder

Instructions:

Combine the ingredients in a high speed blender.

Blend the mixture on high speed for 30 60 seconds until thoroughly combined.

Pour the smoothie into glasses and enjoy immediately.

Nutritional Information:

120 calories per serving, 3.5g fat, 14g carbs, 8.5g protein, 2g fiber

Chocolate Banana Walnut Protein Shake

Servings: 1 o 2

Ingredients:

2 medium frozen bananas, peeled and sliced
1 1/2 cups unsweetened almond milk
1 cup ice cubes
1 scoop chocolate protein powder
1 tablespoon unsweetened cocoa powder

Instructions:

Combine the ingredients in a high-speed blender.

Blend the mixture on high speed for 30 to 60 seconds until thoroughly combined.

Pour the smoothie into glasses and enjoy immediately.

Nutritional Information:

220 calories per serving, 8g fat, 33g carbs, 10g protein, 7g fiber

Cinnamon Almond Protein Shake

Servings: 1 to 2

Ingredients:

1 large frozen banana, peeled and sliced
1 1/2 cups unsweetened almond milk
1/2 cup coconut yogurt
1 scoop plain protein powder
2 tablespoons chopped almonds
1/2 teaspoon ground cinnamon

Instructions:

Combine the ingredients in a high-speed blender.

Blend the mixture on high speed for 30 to 60 seconds until thoroughly combined.

Pour the smoothie into glasses and enjoy immediately.

Nutritional Information:

185 calories per serving, 7.5g fat, 23g carbs, 10g protein, 3.5g fiber

Creamy Orange Dream Protein Shake

Servings: 1 to 2

Ingredients:

1 ripe orange, peeled and chopped
1 1/2 cups unsweetened coconut milk beverage
1 cup coconut yogurt
1/2 cup fresh squeezed orange juice
1 scoop plain protein powder

Instructions:

Combine the ingredients in a high-speed blender.

Blend the mixture on high speed for 30 to 60 seconds until thoroughly combined.

Pour the smoothie into glasses and enjoy immediately.

Nutritional Information:

185 calories per serving, 5g fat, 25g carbs, 9g protein, 2g fiber

Almond Butter Banana Protein Shake

Servings: 1 to 2

Ingredients:

2 medium frozen bananas, peeled and sliced
1 cup coconut yogurt
1/2 cup unsweetened almond milk
1 scoop plain protein powder
2 tablespoons smooth almond butter
3 to 4 drops almond extract

Instructions:

Combine the ingredients in a high-speed blender.

Blend the mixture on high speed for 30 to 60 seconds until thoroughly combined.

Pour the smoothie into glasses and enjoy immediately.

Nutritional Information:

295 calories per serving, 11g fat, 39g carbs, 13g protein, 6g fiber

Additional Notes

Use this section to make additional notes.

THERAPEUTIC SMOOTHIES

Rejuvenating Romaine Raspberry Smoothie

Servings: 1 to 2

Ingredients:
2 cups fresh chopped romaine lettuce
1 1/2 cups frozen raspberries
1 cup coconut water
12 cup unsweetened apple juice
1/2 cup ice cubes
1 tablespoon fresh lime juice

Instructions:
Combine the ingredients in a high speed blender.

Blend the mixture on high speed for 30 to 60 seconds until thoroughly combined.

Pour the smoothie into glasses and enjoy immediately.

Nutritional Information:

265 calories per serving, 0.5g fat, 67g carbs, 2g protein, 6g fiber

Additional Notes

Use this section to make additional notes.

_____

_____

_____

_____

_____

_____

_____

_____

Pick-Me-Up Peach Mango Smoothie

Servings: 1 to 2

Ingredients:
1 1/2 cups frozen sliced peaches
1 cup frozen chopped mango
1 small frozen banana, peeled and sliced
1 cup unsweetened almond milk
1/2 cup coconut water
1/2 cup ice cubes
1 teaspoon coconut oil

Instructions:
Combine the ingredients in a high-speed blender.

Blend the mixture on high speed for 30 to 60 seconds until thoroughly combined.

Pour the smoothie into glasses and enjoy immediately.

Nutritional Information:
180 calories per serving, 4g fat, 38g carbs, 1g protein, 5g fiber

Additional Notes
Use this section to make additional notes.

_____

_____

_____

_____

_____

_____

_____

_____

_____

_____

_____

Immune-Boosting Smoothie

Servings: 1 to 2

Ingredients:
1 pear, medium ripe
1 cup fresh baby spinach, loose leaf
1 teaspoon fresh ginger, grated
1 tablespoon fresh lemon juice
1 cup ice
1 cup water

Instructions:
Rinse the spinach.

Cut pear into chunks.

Combine the spinach, ginger, and lemon in a high-speed blender.

Blend for 20 seconds.

Add pear chunks, water, and ice.

Blend the mixture on high speed for 30-60 seconds until thoroughly combined.

Nutritional Information:

155 calories per serving, 0g fat, 35g carbs, 5g protein

Additional Notes

Use this section to make additional notes.

_____

_____

_____

_____

_____

_____

_____

_____

_____

_____

Calming Cherry Pomegranate Smoothie

Servings: 1 to 2

Ingredients:
1 cup frozen pitted cherries
1 small frozen banana, peeled and sliced
1 cup pomegranate juice, unsweetened
1 cup ice cubes
1/2 cup coconut yogurt
1 tablespoon honey

Instructions:
Combine the ingredients in a high-speed blender.

Blend the mixture on high speed for 30 to 60 seconds until thoroughly combined.

Pour the smoothie into glasses and enjoy immediately.

Nutritional Information:
230 calories per serving, 1g fat, 57g carbs, 2g protein, 3g fiber

Almond and Green Tea Smoothie

Servings: 1 to 2

Ingredients:
1 1/2 cups green tea, brewed and cooled
1 1/2 cups ice cubes
1 cup coconut yogurt
1/4 cup chopped almonds
5 to 6 drops almond extract

Instructions:
Prepare the green tea as a hot tea and allow to cool.

Combine the ingredients in a high-speed blender.

Blend the mixture on high speed for 30 to 60 seconds until thoroughly combined.

Pour the smoothie into glasses and enjoy immediately.

Nutritional Information:
185 calories per serving, 8g fat, 25g carbs, 4.5g protein, 1.5g fiber

Revitalizing Raspberry Cucumber Smoothie

Servings: 1 to 2

Ingredients:
1 1/2 cups frozen raspberries
1 cup seedless cucumber, diced
1 small celery stalk, chopped
1 1/2 cups coconut water
1/2 cups ice cubes
1 tablespoon fresh lemon juice

Instructions:
Combine the ingredients in a high-speed blender.

Blend the mixture on high speed for 30 to 60 seconds until thoroughly combined.

Pour the smoothie into glasses and enjoy.

Nutritional Information:
250 calories per serving, 0.5g fat, 64g carbs, 2g protein, 9g fiber

Energizing Avocado Lime Smoothie

Servings: 1 to 2

Ingredients:
1 ripe avocado, pitted and chopped
1 cup fresh chopped romaine lettuce
1 cup fresh chopped kale
1 1/2 cups unsweetened apple juice
1 cup ice cubes
2 tablespoons fresh lime juice
1 teaspoon fresh lime zest

Instructions:
Combine the ingredients in a high-speed blender.

Blend the mixture on high speed for 30 to 60 seconds until thoroughly combined.

Pour the smoothie into glasses and enjoy.

Nutritional Information:
325 calories per serving, 20g fat, 38.5g carbs, 3.5g protein, 8g fiber

Soothing Cucumber Cantaloupe Cooler

Servings: 1 to 2

Ingredients:
2 cups fresh cantaloupe, peeled and chopped
1 cup seedless cucumber, diced
1 1/2 cups coconut water
1 cup ice cube
2 tablespoons fresh chopped mint
1 tablespoon fresh lime juice

Instructions:
Combine the ingredients in a high-speed blender.

Blend the mixture on high speed for 30 to 60 seconds until thoroughly combined.

Pour the smoothie into glasses and enjoy.

Nutritional Information:
115 calories per serving, 0.5g fat, 28g carbs, 2g protein, 2g fiber

Super Healthy Smoothie

Servings: 1 to 2

Ingredients:
2 large carrots, peeled and chopped
1 large stalk celery, sliced
1 cup fresh baby spinach, chopped
1 cup unsweetened almond milk
1/2 cup fresh-squeezed orange juice
1 to 2 teaspoons fresh minced ginger

Instructions:
Combine the ingredients in a high-speed blender.

Blend the mixture on high speed for 30 to 60 seconds until thoroughly combined.

Pour the smoothie into glasses and enjoy.

Nutritional Information:
110 calories per serving, 2g fat, 22g carbs, 3g protein, 3g fiber

FUN SMOOTHIES

Awesome Apple Ginger Beet Smoothie

Servings: 1 to 2

Ingredients:
1 large ripe apple, cored and chopped
1 medium beet, peeled and chopped
1 small carrot, peeled and chopped
1 cup fresh chopped romaine lettuce
1 cup fresh chopped kale
1 cup unsweetened apple juice
1/2 cup ice cubes
1 teaspoon fresh grated ginger

Instructions:
Combine the ingredients in a high-speed blender.

Blend the mixture on high speed for 30 to 60 seconds until thoroughly combined.

Pour the smoothie into glasses and enjoy.

Nutritional Information:

170 calories per serving, 0.5g fat, 42g carbs, 2.6g protein, 5g fiber

Additional Notes

Use this section to make additional notes.

_____

_____

_____

_____

_____

_____

_____

_____

Merry Mango and Ginger Refresher

Servings: 1 to 2

Ingredients:
2 cups frozen chopped mango
1 small frozen banana, peeled and sliced
1 cup fresh baby spinach, chopped
1 cup fresh-squeezed orange juice
1/2 cup coconut yogurt
1 to 2 teaspoons fresh grated ginger
1 teaspoon fresh lemon juice

Instructions:
Combine the ingredients in a high-speed blender.

Blend the mixture on high speed for 30 to 60 seconds until thoroughly combined.

Pour the smoothie into glasses and enjoy.

Nutritional Information:
240 calories per serving, 1.5g fat, 56g carbs, 4g protein, 4.5g fiber

Cinnamon Pumpkin Pie Smoothie

Servings: 1 to 2

Ingredients:
1 large frozen banana, peeled and sliced
1 cup pumpkin puree
1 cup unsweetened almond milk
1/2 cup ice cubes
1 tablespoon honey
1 teaspoon pumpkin pie spice
5 to 6 drops almond extract

Instructions:
Combine the ingredients in a high-speed blender.

Blend the mixture on high speed for 30 to 60 seconds until thoroughly combined.

Pour the smoothie into glasses and enjoy.

Nutritional Information:
150 calories per serving, 2g fat, 34g carbs, 3g protein, 6.5g fiber

Creamy Cranberry Cinnamon Smoothie

Servings: 1 to 2

Ingredients:
1 cup fresh cranberries
1 large frozen banana, peeled and sliced
1 cup unsweetened almond milk
1/2 cup ice cubes
1/4 teaspoon ground cinnamon

Instructions:
Combine the ingredients in a high-speed blender.

Blend the mixture on high speed for 30 to 60 seconds until thoroughly combined.

Pour the smoothie into glasses and enjoy.

Nutritional Information:
115 calories per serving, 2g fat, 22g carbs, 1g protein, 4g fiber

Wacky Watermelon Refresher

Servings: 1 to 2

Ingredients:
2 cups frozen chopped watermelon
1 cup frozen sliced strawberries
1/2 cup coconut yogurt
1/2 cup coconut water
1/4 cup fresh squeezed orange juice
1 tablespoon fresh lemon juice

Instructions:
Combine the ingredients in a high-speed blender.

Blend the mixture on high speed for 30 to 60 seconds until thoroughly combined.

Pour the smoothie into glasses and enjoy.

Nutritional Information:
140 calories per serving, 1.5g fat, 31.5g carbs, 2.5g protein, 2g fiber

Velvety Vanilla Almond Smoothie

Servings: 1 to 2

Ingredients:
2 medium frozen bananas, peeled and sliced
1 1/2 cups unsweetened vanilla almond milk
1 cup coconut yogurt
2 tablespoons chopped almonds
1/4 teaspoon vanilla extract

Instructions:
Combine the ingredients in a high-speed blender.

Blend the mixture on high speed for 30 to 60 seconds until thoroughly combined.

Pour the smoothie into glasses and enjoy.

Nutritional Information:
230 calories per serving, 7g fat, 38g carbs, 5.5g protein, 6g fiber

Crazy Cucumber Melon Cooler

Servings: 1 to 2

Ingredients:
1 medium seedless cucumber, chopped
1 cup fresh honeydew, peeled and chopped
1 cup coconut water
1/2 cup ice cube
2 tablespoons fresh chopped mint
1 tablespoon fresh lime juice

Instructions:
Combine the ingredients in a high-speed blender.

Blend the mixture on high speed for 30 to 60 seconds until thoroughly combined.

Pour the smoothie into glasses and enjoy.

Nutritional Information:
90 calories per serving, 0.5g fat, 23g carbs, 2g protein, 2g fiber

Blackberry Yogurt Smoothie with Mint

Servings: 1 to 2

Ingredients:
2 cups frozen blackberries
1 small frozen banana, peeled and sliced
1 cup coconut water
1/2 cup unsweetened apple juice
1/4 cup fresh mint

Instructions:
Combine the ingredients in a high-speed blender.

Blend the mixture on high speed for 30 to 60 seconds until thoroughly combined.

Pour the smoothie into glasses and enjoy.

Nutritional Information:
195 calories per serving, 3g fat, 40.5g carbs, 5g protein, 10g fiber

Additional Notes

Use this section to make additional notes.

_____

_____

_____

_____

_____

_____

_____

_____

_____

_____

_____

CONCLUSION

Whether you are trying to lose weight, improve your health, or just make healthy changes to your diet, the Pegan Diet is an excellent option. A combination of the Paleo Diet and Vegan Diet, coupled with a few changes made to include gluten-free grains and small amounts of grass-fed meats, eggs, and seafood makes this an excellent diet for today's busy, stressful world. If you think this diet lifestyle might be right for you, this cookbook is the perfect place to begin. Simply choose a recipe from this book and get started! You will not be disappointed. Then grab the other cookbooks in the *Pegan Pantry Diet Cookbook* series.

Yes, You've Done It!

Congratulations! You've made it to the end of this cookbook. I hope this is only the beginning of an adventure for you into a whole new lifestyle with an emphasis on clean eating and a healthy lifestyle.

Get Your Free Pegan Food Pantry Checklist

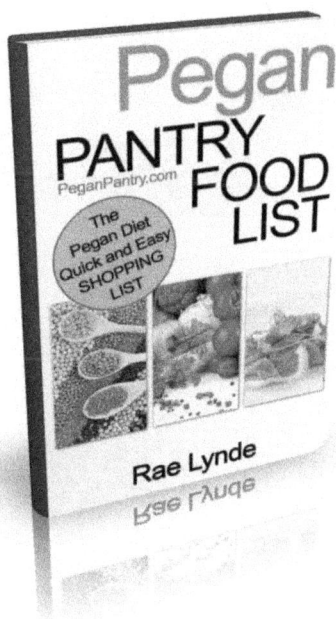

FREE PEGAN PANTRY FOOD LIST
The Pegan Diet Quick and Easy Shopping List
Go to: www.PeganPantry.com

My Pegan Diet Cookbooks:

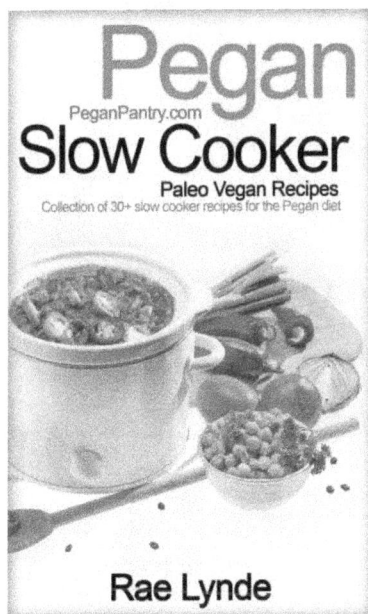

Pegan
PeganPantry.com
Slow Cooker
Paleo Vegan Recipes
Collection of 30+ slow cooker recipes for the Pegan diet

Rae Lynde

PEGAN SLOWCOOKER RECIPES

30+ mouthwatering recipes that will save you time. These good clean eating, delicious, quick and easy slow-cooker recipes are gluten-free and dairy-free. You'll find recipes for breakfast, dinner, soups and stews, and dessert recipes, all for one-pot slow cooking.

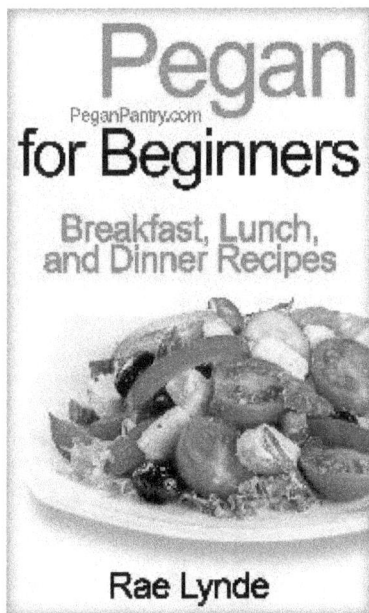

Pegan
PeganPantry.com
for Beginners
Breakfast, Lunch,
and Dinner Recipes

Rae Lynde

PEGAN for BEGINNERS

Better Health, High Energy, and Weight Loss
45 Pegan Diet Recipes for Beginners. The Pegan diet offers many health and weight loss benefits. Recipes include those for breakfast, lunch, dinner, desserts, and snacks.

About the Author

Rae Lynde loves food, enjoys cooking, and lives to find ways to combine good food and good health. When she's not in the kitchen or pouring over recipe books, she's reading, gardening, and writing. She enjoys growing her own herbs and vegetables, too.

Enjoyed this Cookbook?

I hope you've enjoyed this collection of smoothie recipes and hope you let others know about the Pegan Diet and my cookbooks. Like every other author, I do my best to put together a book that my readers will enjoy and find helpful.

One feature you may enjoy more and more as time goes by are the blank lined pages in the paperback editions. (Technology has not made it possible to do that for eBooks)

Your feedback is crucial to the success of authors like me who are helped by the readers who have read, enjoyed, and found their books useful or helpful, and who are then happy to let others know. If you have enjoyed this book, I'd be grateful if you would take a few minutes to leave an honest review on Amazon or wherever you either bought the book or wherever you enjoy sharing your reading experiences.

Thank you!

Rae Lynde

NOTES

_____

_____

_____

_____

_____

_____

_____

_____

_____

_____

_____

_____

_____

_____

_____

INDEX

ABOUT SMOOTHIES 9

What Are Smoothies? 9

What Are Their Benefits? 9

Why are Pegan smoothies good for you? 10

What equipment do you need? 11

How to get started 11

PEGAN DIET BASICS 13

Five Health Benefits of the Pegan Diet 14

Eight Ways to Avoid or Reduce Animal Fat 14

What you Need to Do for Smoothies 16

WHY I LOVE PEGAN 1

SMOOTHIE RECIPES 5

FRUIT SMOOTHIES 9

Refreshing Raspberry Smoothie 9

Terrific Triple Berry Blend 11

Tropical Mango Pineapple Smoothie 12

Bountiful Blueberry Mint Blend 13

Peachy Pear Mango Smoothie 14

Sweet Strawberry Kiwi Smoothie 15

Double Berry Blast with Coconut 16

Bright Carrot Cucumber and Pear Smoothie 17

GREEN SMOOTHIES 21

Sassy Spinach Green Apple Smoothie 21

Spinach Avocado Lime Cooler 23

Celery Cucumber and Kale Smoothie 24

Gorgeous Green Grape Smoothie 25

Zippy Zucchini Kiwi Smoothie 26

Cucumber Kale Green Smoothie 27

Broccoli Cucumber Blast 28

Invigorating Kiwi Kale Smoothie 29

Celery Spinach and Cucumber Smoothie 30

BANANA SMOOTHIES 33

Simple Strawberry Banana Smoothie 33

Coco-Nutty Banana Smoothie 35

Easy Almond Butter Banana Smoothie 36

Bangin' Banana Yogurt Smoothie 37

Perfect Pineapple Banana Smoothie 38

Blueberry Banana Blend with Lime 39

PROTEIN SMOOTHIES 43

Choco-Coconut Protein Shake 43

Smooth Strawberry Yogurt Protein Shake 45

Chocolate Banana Walnut Protein Shake 46

Cinnamon Almond Protein Shake 47

Creamy Orange Dream Protein Shake 48

Almond Butter Banana Protein Shake 49

THERAPEUTIC SMOOTHIES 53

Rejuvenating Romaine Raspberry Smoothie 53

Pick-Me-Up Peach Mango Smoothie 55

Immune-Boosting Smoothie 57

Calming Cherry Pomegranate Smoothie 59

Almond and Green Tea Smoothie 60

Revitalizing Raspberry Cucumber Smoothie 61

Energizing Avocado Lime Smoothie 62

Soothing Cucumber Cantaloupe Cooler 63

Super Healthy Smoothie 64

FUN SMOOTHIES 67

Awesome Apple Ginger Beet Smoothie 67

Merry Mango and Ginger Refresher 69

Cinnamon Pumpkin Pie Smoothie 70

Creamy Cranberry Cinnamon Smoothie 71

Wacky Watermelon Refresher 72

Velvety Vanilla Almond Smoothie 73

Crazy Cucumber Melon Cooler 74

Blackberry Yogurt Smoothie with Mint 75

CONCLUSION 79

Yes, You've Done It! 81

Get Your Free Pegan Food Pantry Checklist 81

My Pegan Diet Cookbooks: 83

About the Author 87

Enjoyed this Cookbook? 89

NOTES 91

INDEX 107

*9 7 8 1 9 4 1 3 0 3 2 6 9 *